WHATEVER HAPPENED TO THE ORPHAN JOSEPH GARDNER?

WHATEVER HAPPENED TO THE ORPHAN JOSEPH GARDNER?

James A. Ryals and Carol S. Ryals

authorHOUSE®

AuthorHouse™ LLC
1663 Liberty Drive
Bloomington, IN 47403
www.authorhouse.com
Phone: 1-800-839-8640

Published by AuthorHouse   01/17/2014

ISBN: 978-1-4918-5440-2 (sc)
ISBN: 978-1-4918-5554-6 (e)

Library of Congress Control Number: 2014901239

Maude Ryals, James' mother

IN MEMORY OF POWELL
AND
MAUDE RYALS

CHILDHOOD

March 17, 1932! A baby boy was born to Ann Gardner in Tampa Florida! Whatever reason she had, she made the decision to leave the baby at the Tampa Orphanage. It really didn't matter why she could not keep the child. The main thing was her concern for the child's welfare and felt the Tampa Orphanage was her best choice.

It was around April, 1932, that Maude and Powell Ryals were sitting around the breakfast table in Zephyrhills, Florida discussing whether they should contact the Tampa Orphanage in an attempt to adopt a child. They had lost their only child at birth several years ago and Maude felt she wasn't able to carry another child at her age since she was already 49 years old. She wanted to have a child for Powell to carry on his name and have grandchildren.

They decided to visit the orphanage to talk to the director and meet some of the children. They called that day for an appointment with the director, Dr. Cobb. The next day at 10 A.M. they met with him to see about their chances of adopting one of the children. Dr. Cobb said, "There are three primary things the board will consider prior to an adoption: [1] The age of the adoptive parents is a concern, [2] Whether the applicants can afford to care for the child, and [3] Are they respected in their community and will they love the child."

In June they made their first visit to meet some of the older children, in fact, they ended up spending the whole day there. Toward the end of the visit Dr. Cobb took them to see the babies, pointing to one baby in particular in a crib across the room. He mentioned this little boy had arrived recently and was named Joseph.

While Maude held him she noticed he had a dimple in his chin just like she had. "Powell! Do you see that dimple in the baby's chin?"

"Yes, it's kind of cute and it looks just like yours."

Maude immediately felt a bond with this child. So she asked, "Dr. Cobb, what is the history of this baby and is he in good health?"

The Director told them the baby had been born on March 17th and assured them he was in excellent health. He couldn't give them much background on the baby because the mother requested no information be revealed.

"Thank you for giving us the opportunity of visiting with all these wonderful children. Powell and I will need to talk about what age of child we would like to complete our household. We are going to have lots to discuss and will get back to you in the near future. Thanks again to your staff for being so kind."

Dr. Cobb escorted the Ryals to the door and said, "Call any time or just come on back if you have any questions. Goodbye and have a good day."

They talked about the baby Joseph all the way home. At one point mom looked at Powell and asked him, "Powell do you really want to adopt a child, especially a little baby?"

He looked at Maude with tears in his eyes and said, "I am sure that little baby will capture my heart."

Two days had passed by when suddenly mom said, "Powell get your shoes on and let's go back to orphanage!"

Maude and Powell returned to the Tampa Orphanage where the guard escorted them to the office and they asked to see the Director. A few minutes later Dr. Cobb came out of his office and shook their hands. He invited them into his office and told them to have a seat. Maude said, "Dr. Cobb, Powell and I have been excited about Joseph ever since we were here the other day. How do we start the process of adopting him?"

Dr. Cobb said, "I have made some inquiries since we first met. I found out you folks have a successful business in Zephyrhills, and you both are members of the First Baptist Church. I see, Maude, you are active in the Women's Club and both of you count votes after the elections. I understand, Powell, you are currently Master of the local Masonic Lodge and you had an honorable discharge from the Army after World War I. Also neither of you are smokers or drinkers. Folks, are my facts correct?"

Mom answered for both of them. "Yes, all those facts are correct."

"Good, I will present my recommendation to the board for their approval. Maude, you and Powell check back with me after 10 A.M. tomorrow and I will have an answer for you."

After that they went to visit baby Joseph and stayed for about a couple of hours, giving him his bottle, holding and playing with him. Maude even had the chance to change his diapers a couple of times. Powell enjoyed holding him and walking around the room with him until they finally had to leave so they both kissed him goodbye.

Before they left Tampa they stopped at Kress Department store to pick up a few additional clothes just for a baby boy and more diapers. They could never have too many diapers.

On the way home Maude asked Powell, "Have you thought of a name for the baby?"

"Yes, I would like to call him James but don't know what we should use for a middle name. I don't want to call him Powell! Do you have any suggestions?"

Maude answered, "I have been thinking about the name Arthur, because then his initials would spell JAR and that would mean he will be lucky."

Without any hesitation dad said, "JAMES ARTHUR RYALS. Yes, that sounds good to me."

Mom replied, "Sounds good to me too."

The last sixteen hours had seemed like a week! Mom and dad were excited about having the opportunity to have a son. After breakfast, mom told dad, "Get the lead out. We are going to Tampa! I don't even want to wait to call."

They arrived around 9:45 A.M. and went straight to the Director's office. His secretary knew about the Ryals and said, "Good morning, Mr. and Mrs. Ryals, I will tell Dr. Cobb you are here." She went into the Director's office and told him the Ryals were waiting. Dr. Cobb told her to send them in. After greeting them Dr. Cobb said, "The board and I want to welcome you into our family and congratulate you two on having a new son." They shook hands and then he told them, "See Nancy, my secretary, and she will help you complete the required forms. Goodbye and congratulations."

They left his office and sat down at Nancy's desk. Mom asked her, "What information do you want from us?" Nancy went over the forms and after they had completed them, she had them sign the papers. She excused herself and took the forms to Dr. Cobb for his signature. She returned shortly with the signed forms and handed them to Mrs. Ryals. Nancy then proceeded to explain what the next procedure was to change the baby's name. After it was all over Nancy said, "Congratulations! If you have any problems feel free to call me. Now go get your new son!"

Maude and Powell were so excited as they headed toward the nursery to get their new son. Mom picked me up and gave me a big kiss, then handed me to dad while she gathered my clothes, diapers, etc. They got in their truck and headed for our home in Zephyrhills. According to the time line when I reached five months old I would officially be a Ryals.

The Ryals currently owned and operated a Dry Goods and Grocery Store. When James turned one year old they sold their business and home. Then they purchased a larger house and also opened a new business in the center of town called: POWELL RYAL'S FURNITURE EXCHANGE. Powell was dad's middle name and everyone in the community called him Powell and it made sense to use his name in the store title.

When I was five years old mother decided to start my education and enrolled me in Mrs. Baxter's Kindergarten class. During the 1930s kindergarten was an option and only available in a private school. These classes were in the morning Monday through Friday. But after only two weeks, Mrs. Baxter told Mom, "Please keep James (I was always called James not Jim) home because he disrupts the other students." That was the end of my kindergarten days! Normally I was a good kid but my biggest problem was talking rather than listening.

Mrs. Hamilton, my first grade teacher, sent me to the corner numerous times for interrupting her class. I am sure she didn't miss me when the next year I could make the second grade teacher, Mrs. Ford, miserable.

It was around this age we went visiting one evening at a friend's house. When I walked into their house their Great Dane dog lunged at me and bit me on the face. He seemed to think I was a threat to his mistress. My poor mom got real upset and the hostess was horrified that her dog would do this. After a while everyone settled down including the dog. Fortunately it wasn't a serious bite.

My mother was an accomplished pianist and we always had a quality piano in our house. One day mom said, "James, I need to teach you how to play the piano!"

"I don't want to play the piano, mother!" I guess she didn't hear me or just ignored me because I was directed to the piano and started my first lesson. First it was learning the scales. So I practiced an hour every day for a week. I was doing okay while mom was sitting next to me but when she left me to keep up the practice, I goofed off. My mind was thinking about playing with the other kids. So finally my mother decided it was a waste of time and let me off the hook.

Zephyrhills has two one-way streets that are separated by a big island. This is 5th Avenue where the street on one side of the island runs west to east and the other side runs east to west. This island starts at the west side of town by the city park and continues for approximately one mile to the east side of town. The main part of downtown is four blocks long with parking on both sides. This island is about fourteen feet wide which was filled with dirt and in some places there were small trees growing. Often some of the kids would play marbles in the dirt.

When I was about six years old, Bobby Wells and I were fussing during a marble game and we were getting mad at each other like kids do. I made some wise comment to Bobby and he stood up and said, "James, you think because your dad owns a business that you can boss us around." Then he made this comment, "Well at least I am not adopted!"

That upset me because I did not know what adopted meant and he made it sound like something bad. He had hurt my feelings and I ran crying into our store. I saw mother over at the desk and said, "Mother, what does adopted mean? Bobby said I was adopted."

Mom replied, "James, your father and I planned on telling you about being adopted when we felt you were old enough to understand. I guess that time has come!" Then she explained about adoption and told me I should be proud because "we picked you to be our son. When we first saw you our hearts told us God had sent you to us and we are so happy."

I stopped crying immediately because I knew my parents loved me and I was special because they 'picked me'. I felt like the luckiest kid in town. When I saw Bobby again I thanked him for telling me I was adopted.

When I was in the third grade dad asked me, "James would you like to listen to the big heavyweight fight tonight?"

"Sure would Dad!"

So that evening my dad took me down to the furniture store where several of his lodge brothers were waiting for him. The Joe Lewis [BROWN BOMBER] Heavy Weight Fight was going to be broadcast on the radio at 7 P.M. All of the men grabbed a chair and gathered in a circle. They had their cigarettes, cigars, pipes and bottles of coke. Dad kept the bottles of coke cold in a refrigerator at the back of the store. Dad had me lie down on a couch during the fight but I never knew why. It soon became a ritual for me to be there. Sometimes I would fall asleep and miss the outcome of the fight. I cannot remember whether everyone was a Lewis fan or if some of them wanted the other fighter to win. The most important point about this time was the fellowship these men had with each other and I was a part of it. It made me feel so grown up.

Sometimes dad and several of his lodge buddies would go out with a big flashlight at night to the Hillsborough River swamp and hunt for small or baby alligators. Mom didn't appreciate him bringing home baby alligators which he kept in an old Coca Cola chest style machine. I was not allowed to go along. My dad could go out where there were lots of mosquitoes in those swamps but he never got bit. That's because dad had a little Seminole Indian in his blood. He was quite a horseman too but at a local race a few years earlier he was thrown from his horse at the finish line. He was unconscious for a couple of days and it affected his mobility over the years.

My dad and I would go to the small lakes and fish and many times would go swimming. Dad taught me how to swim in a local lake. The first time he threw me into the lake and said "swim or drown". I started swimming under water until my dad grabbed me and pulled me out. Then he taught me how to swim on top of the water. I knew he wouldn't let me drown.

The WPA built a large swimming pool and roller skating rink down in the park. This area is where the "Yankees" from the north came for the winter. They all had nice trailers and camped out all winter. There were usually around forty trailers at any one time. They were mostly retired folks and they normally socialized among themselves.

Most of the local children took advantage of the pool and rink. My folks allowed me swim in the pool without their supervision because there were two life guards on duty all the time. The city was proud of their nice pool and they kept it clean and well managed.

I had never roller skated before but several of us kids decided we would learn how. My buddies and I got many bruises before we learned how to stay off the floor. We finally were able to enjoy this activity without spending so much time on the floor and went often. I also learned a couple of years later how to be a skate boy and put on the customers skates. These were the old style skates that clamped on your shoes and were tightened by a skate key. I got free skating for doing this.

Work was hard to find all over the country around 1940 and the Seaboard Railroad Line which was located about two blocks east of our house appeared to be a favorite place for the hobos jumping off the train as it entered town. We had a couple of these men stop and knock on our back door almost weekly. Mother always found some food for each one. She never turned away anyone that was hungry. Sometimes she would have them do a minor task for her but she would feed them whether they worked or not. Sometimes I felt the word was passed among the hobos that you could always get something to eat at our house.

I was in the third grade when news came over the radio about Pearl Harbor, on December 7,

1941. Since I was just a young child the impact of this news did not register.

The Mayor of Zephyrhills immediately called a town meeting when he heard the news to decide how we could assist the military and provide some protection for our small town. At the meeting was a retired WW I Army Air Force major by the name of Charles Bond. He stood up to address the group of concerned citizens about the potential hazards during war time. He suggested a large bomb shelter should be built in the middle of town. They should also build a forty foot tower to be used by aircraft movement spotters who would phone the information to a command post. This tower would be manned by volunteers during daylight hours only.

The Mayor was impressed with Mr. Bond's ideas and asked him if he would be interested in being in charge of town security. Charles replied, "It will be an honor to be of service to my country again." The whole country was in a panic mood and young men stood in long lines trying to enlist. Even some of the older men tried to join the service.

A couple of weeks after the meeting both the bomb shelter and the tower construction was started. The Mayor decided to have them built side by side adjacent to the large band stand in the center of the town.

This is the location where we set up a large Christmas tree every year and Santa would hand out fruit and candy to all the children of the surrounding community each Christmas. Also the band stand was used by candidates to give speeches for various political offices and several times a year the Zephyrhills band would give a concert. Across the street were several shuffleboard courts where people could come and play shuffleboard any time during the day. There was always something going on.

I can remember playing with my friends in the shelter after it was built and sometimes we would climb up the long flight of stairs to where the spotters stood searching the sky with binoculars for planes. The planes in those days were only the propeller type and could easily be identified with help from a chart showing the different types of aircraft. The volunteers plotted the planes course and relayed by phone to the command post the type of plane, its position, and which direction it was flying. The volunteers are retired men and rotate every three hours during daylight hours.

It was during the war when I was in the fifth grade the school collected scrap metal to sell and the proceeds were used for the benefit of the school. Anyone could donate scrap and the pile grew to about ten feet tall and fifty feet in diameter. There was also food ration stamps and gas rationing. The gas rationing made it difficult for dad because of his buying trips and his delivery of furniture.

During my growing up years one of the activities we boys liked to do was go about two miles out of town and play soldier in the woods. Usually there were about ten of us ages eight to twelve. We would choose up sides and play war. One side was U.S. Army and the other was the enemy. We would allow about thirty minutes for the enemy team to head for the brush and hide. If we caught someone all we had to do was touch them and they were out of the game. While we were out in the woods we would look for Rabbit Tobacco plants and make cigars with the brown paper from sacks. We actually smoked the stuff and sometimes we got sick. I guess we were trying to act grown up.

In the rainy season our city park and the lake would flood. Sometimes the water came all the way up to the pool area. Most of the guys could swim so we went down to the park and climbed up the big oak trees to jump in the water. I guess we didn't think about snakes but at least there were no alligators! Normally we skinny dipped when we were in an area away from houses. You can understand why!

When the weather was good we played sandlot baseball and football. We had a super time and enjoyed life. Once in a while a couple of us got mad and shoved and yelled but there was not much hitting.

Early in March 1942, dad was diagnosed with Parkinson's disease. As the disease progressed over the years it became difficult for him to run the store and he spent most of the time on a cot at the rear of the store. When a customer would come in the store he would tell them to look around and if they found something they wanted to buy dad would handle the money. The community knew about dads condition and because dad was well respected and it was a small town everyone was very cooperative.

Mom started to spend more time in the store with dad. If an item was sold and required delivery she usually found old Jack to assist her in the delivery. Jack lived with his parents and did odd jobs around town. Mom paid him 75 cents for each piece of merchandise that he assisted us in delivering. Mother started handling all the buying trips to Tampa for the purpose of filling orders for new furniture, linoleum, mattresses, etc. Usually dad had made those trips and did the buying, but due to his poor health mother took over the responsibility. She would take me out of school for the day to go along with her.

I really enjoyed those trips because we would visit the mattress and furniture factories, and the stores that sold linoleum at whole sale. After putting in the orders for the merchandise at each location we would go to Maas Cafeteria to eat, the only cafeteria in town. I was given a metal tray which I pushed along a counter and selected items on display that I wanted from the many wonderful looking things to eat. The server would put those items on my tray and I would feel so grown up to be able to pick out what I wanted. At the end of the counter a cashier would total up the cost for the items you selected and you would pay her for your food. Mother always told me how much I could spend so I kept a running figure in my head of the cost of the items I selected to insure that I would not spend too much.

After eating we would get into the truck and head for the various places we had purchased merchandise. They would load up the merchandise on our 1938 Chevy pickup. Sometimes we would pay on the spot and other times they gave us 30 days to pay.

Dad had built side rails by attaching boards to four posts that fit down in the holes on the bed of the truck. This helped increase our hauling space and then we would tie everything down with strong ropes. We had no canvas to cover the merchandise so we had to keep a look out for rain. Since the speed limit was only 35mph it took a while to reach home. If it started to rain we would try to find cover. Sometimes we pulled the truck into the shed at the prison road camp near Zephyrhills. The prisoners were all on the Trustee program and always wanted to help mom.

Zephyrhills is a farm town and the Ryals kept the store open on Saturday night like most all of the retail businesses. The doors closed at 9 P.M. except on Wednesdays when most stores closed at 1 P.M. After the folks closed at nine on Saturday the three of us went to the Brent hog farm which was about two miles north of town. There the folks played pinochle until midnight. I would sit on dad's lap to help him handle the cards and that was how I learned the game. After they played for a while there was always cake or pie to eat. Usually after I ate I lay down on the couch and fell asleep while they continued playing. Once when we were out at the farm during the day I climbed the fence into the hog pen. A big old boar charged after me but fortunately Farmer Brent was there. He took a big stick and beat the hog off. Farmer Brent severely chastised me and told me never ever do that again. Sometimes hogs can be very dangerous.

Occasionally on Sunday morning mom and I would go to the Methodist church when she would be asked to play the organ for them. Otherwise I attended First Baptist Church.

One of the two drug stores would always be open from 1 P.M. to 4 P.M. on Sunday but all other retail stores including gas stations were closed. This way medicine could be provided if needed.

We had a fire department that was all volunteers and since it was such a small town even some teenage boys helped out. When I got older I helped out too but we mostly were asked to help put out grass fires. There was only one policeman in Zephyrhills for many years. Since there was very little trouble in town he just made sure everyone continued behaving themselves. We also had two railroads, the Seaboard that went through the center of town and the Atlantic Coastline that went on the east side of town.

In the summer season on Sunday sometimes a plane would fly over in the afternoon and buzz the town to let the folks know if they wanted to have a ride they should come out to a big old pasture west of town. When there were about 25 people gathered the pilots would offer to take two people at a time for $3.00 a person and make a short flight over the town. I was never able to ride because of a lack of money but I loved watching.

One night at about 3 o'clock in the morning my mother came upstairs to my room and said, "James, wake up! There is a big fire up town. I can see the glow from our front porch. Come with me. Let's go up the street and see where it is." I was still half asleep but went with her anyway. It was the hotel which eventually burned to the ground that night. This hotel was located on the corner of State Highway 301 and the main street of town. It was never rebuilt but there was another hotel downtown. This one had the only eating place in town other than sandwiches at the two drug stores and the bus stop which was located at a gas station.

Life was good and James was the typical boy in that period of time. Growing up in Zephyrhills in the 40s was a life many children in these modern days can't begin to fathom. I had freedom to roam and play without supervision and learned to make up my own games and use my imagination. I loved to fish, swim and play all sports.

One time my folks took me out in the woods about four miles from town to fish in this one creek. During this period there weren't many fences to block our way because of the 'open range policy'. Dad and I took off down the creek in one direction and mom went the other way. We hadn't gotten 50 feet when we heard mom screaming and hollering for help. Of course we took off in her direction and there was mom stuck up to her waist in quicksand. We began to laugh and mom becoming a little perturbed demanded, "Aren't you going to pull me out?" We immediately got some big branches and pulled her up to solid ground. After the three of us settled down on the bank of the creek, we all started to laugh! Mom looked a mess with mud all over her. She decided to wash off in the creek and sat in the sun to dry off. When she was reasonably dry we went to the truck to get the fried chicken, potato salad, and some cold ice tea. We spread a blanket on the ground and had an old fashioned southern picnic!

After we ate we decided to call it a day and headed home. We didn't feel like fishing anymore and I think that was the last time we went fishing in that particular area.

When dad and I did bring home a mess of fish, we had to clean them out on the back porch. Mom would cook them but would not clean them! Once dad took me with him out on a deep sea fishing boat that went out into the Gulf about thirty miles. I had a great time watching the charter guests pulling in large fish weighing ten pounds or more. The crew cleaned these fish, iced them, and every one of the group took home their share. That was a great experience and I really enjoyed doing things with my dad.

My father was born on a farm and loved the country. Several times when I was between the ages of six and ten he took me hunting. Normally he shot rabbits and squirrels and they would make some good eating especially if mom fried them.

A friend of my dad loved to hunt gophers [land turtles]. They looked like the turtles that live in the water but they live down in a hole in the sandy portion of the woods. They only ate grass and traveled on dry land. These hard shelled animals are called gophers in the southeastern states. The only part of this animal used for food are their legs which are skinned and deep fried. It takes the legs of at least four large gophers to make a meal for two people.

One day dad's friend took me out to the wooded area west of town where cattle were grazing and the soil was real sandy. He had a long pole with a wire hook on the end that he ran down a gopher (land turtle) hole. Sometimes he pulled out a gopher and other times a snake.

The snake usually lived in the holes with the animals. Of course if the snake was poisonous he would kill it otherwise he just chased it away. After he caught four or more large gophers we headed for the "barn" (home).

Another food that came direct from nature was skunk cabbage and was called 'poor mans food'. This was the heart of a palmetto tree that grew in sandy areas. The tree would be cut down and the heart boiled with ham hock for seasoning. It smelled like a skunk and my mother refused to cook it but I was told it was good eating.

On July fourth in my tenth year, mom told me that we were going to Uncle Cleve's for a big bar-b-que on his ranch in Pasco County for the Ryals family. Uncle Cleve owned a 500 acre cattle ranch twenty miles northeast of Zephyrhills. When we arrived at the ranch entrance I had to get out of the truck and open the gate and after the truck drove through I had to close it again. Then we had to drive on a sandy road for another three miles before reaching the ranch house. Mom explained that the house was for the foreman and his family since Uncle Cleve and his family lived in Tampa.

The bar-b-que pit was a big hole in the ground with a piece of mesh-like wire fencing across the top and was located about fifty feet from the ranch house. One of the ranch hands was in charge of cooking the meat.

Someone inquired, "What kind of meat are we having?"

The ranch hand replied, "There is wild turkey, pig, beef, chicken, deer and rabbit. Anything you want."

My dad was born into a large family of seven boys and seven girls with dad being the youngest. I had only met about half of the family. They lived all over with some of them living in Tampa, Plant City, Zephyrhills, etc. Someone said there was only about fifty of them here today.

I do remember some of the families like: Uncle Dee & Uncle Cleve who both owned large livestock sale barns in Tampa, Uncle Jeff owned a large dairy farm east of Tampa, Aunt Ruth was from Plant City, Aunt Barbara (her husband was a preacher) and family were from Tampa. There were several other relatives I didn't know. All of dad's brothers dealt in livestock except him. He was a merchant.

After we all had eaten way too much the men played horse shoes while the women sat around and talked. There were a lot of children there so I had fun playing games with them.

There was also a large fenced in arena near the barn used for training horses where they had four saddled horses for us kids to ride. It was such an enjoyable day and we went home tired and happy.

One incident that happened that summer was when my dad took to me visit a friend who had been a German research professor in Berlin, Germany. He and his wife escaped from Germany early in the war and fled to Zephyrhills. Shortly after their arrival she passed away. When we went into his house that day there in the living room was a glass casket with his dead wife in it. She had been dead about two years. That scared me to death! Most of the people in town considered him extremely strange. There was even a story written in a detective mystery magazine about this gentleman.

One Sunday morning late in the summer I decided to hitchhike to Tampa where the Florida State Fair was in progress. I didn't tell the folks because I knew they would not let me go. Instead I told them I was going to Sunday School and then play with some of my friends. I told my mom, "Don't worry about lunch."

I had about $5.00 in my pocket and knew that would be sufficient. So I walked down to Hwy 301 and stuck out my thumb. When a car stopped I inquired if they were going to Tampa and if so could I get a ride. Using your thumb on the highway was accepted during the early 40s. I arrived in Tampa and they dropped me off near one of the trolley routes. For 10 cents I could ride all over town so I took the trolley to the fairgrounds and for 25 cents got in the gate. I walked around the midway and then went into the barns to see the 4-H livestock. When I got hungry I had a hot dog and soda for fifteen cents. I lost track of time and suddenly noticed it was getting late so I asked someone what time it was. When they told me it was two o'clock I panicked. I needed to head back to Zephyrhills.

I took a trolley out to the Produce Market so I could see if one of the truckers would give me a lift. I talked to about fifteen truckers but none of them were going through Zephyrhills. By this time it was around 4:30 P.M. and I knew my folks would start to worry. There was a Highway Patrol Office next to the market so I went in and talked to the patrolman on duty. I explained to him my situation and started crying. He contacted the patrol working in the Zephyrhills area and asked if they would meet them at the county line to take me home. They agreed so I thanked the Tampa patrolman for making the arrangements. The Pasco County Patrol Officer met us at the county line and took me home. On the way he chastised me for hitchhiking at such a young age. He told me how dangerous it could be. I thanked him for taking time to help me and promised not to hitchhike again. Then I went inside the house and confronted my mother.

When I told her what had happened she became very upset with me. She got the yard stick and said, "James Arthur! You're going to get a spanking for lying to me and doing something so foolish! You know dad and I were worried to death about you. Come here."

It was rare for mom to spank me. She was so upset and worried about me that she just lost her cool. That was the last time I did that again! (And by the way the spanking hurt.)

When I was eleven years old my mother had dad close the store for a week and took me to Cartersville, Georgia, north of Atlanta. There was a resort on a big lake with cabins and an old country store where you could buy supplies. The lake was used for swimming and boating. The swimming area even had diving boards. The local people that lived there year around had small structures built over the cold creeks for storing melons, eggs, etc. in the water to keep them cool. I spent a joyous week swimming, boating and fishing with my parents. But all too soon it was time to go home.

On our return trip home mom made a stop in Atlanta to buy peaches. We still had our 1938 Chevy pickup with just one seat for three people and a stick shift on the floor. She loaded the baskets of fruit in the back of the pickup with our suitcases. When we got home she sent me around town selling bags of peaches which paid for our trip. Did I mention my mother knew how to make a buck!

Everything was rationed during the war and gas was difficult to obtain without coupons. We parked our truck in a garage behind our house which was at least 40 feet from our back door. One night my mother was awakened by a noise coming from the back of our house. She got me up and we took a flashlight along when we headed for the garage. Someone was in the garage trying to siphon the gas out of our pickup! Mother let out a yell and recognizing the man in the flashlight beam, I yelled, "Mom! That man is Mr. Brown!" Well he took off running leaving the can on the ground. I never heard what mom ever did about that event.

One afternoon while I was in our store dad said to me, "James, I would like you to go with me to the Joe Harris farm tonight after I close the store and we will spend the night. Joe and his family went on vacation for a week and I told him that I would look after his place and the livestock."

The farm was about three miles southwest of town on a small lake. He had some chickens and pigs that needed to be fed. There was no electricity so we used a lantern and a battery radio. There was no running water either but there was an outhouse behind the house. Now I am a city boy and never used an outhouse before so this was a new experience. When I went out there the smell was really bad! I can say thank goodness we live in town with indoor plumbing. I told dad, "Dad unless you really need me I had rather not spend another night on this farm."

Dad gave a big laugh and said, "Okay, you are excused, you city slicker."

It was also during this time on a bright sunny day I was walking around town seeing if I could find any of my friends to hang out with. I saw a man in a strange uniform sitting on one of the benches. Since I did not recognize him my first words to him were, "Mister, do you need any help?"

He replied, "No, I am just traveling through town on the way back to the port in Tampa. I am from the Russian ship docked there."

I was surprised he spoke reasonably good English. "What is your name, mister?"

"It is Frederick. What is your name?"

"James. Welcome to our town."

"Well James, I am pleased to meet you. I have been traveling around the area a little and find this a real nice town."

"Thank you, and you have a good trip back to Tampa. I must be going now."

"Thank you James, and goodbye."

The Army Air Force constructed a base just southeast of town for the purpose of training fighter pilots for the 8th Air Force. The GIs spent their off duty time at our roller rink, swimming pool, movie house and kept the drug store sandwich shops busy. There was really not much for them to do in this small town with only a population of 1500. I was real friendly to these soldiers so they were always buying ice cream or candy for me which I didn't mind. But my mother found out and told me to stop taking hand outs and I should earn money to buy treats if I wanted them. So I decided to start shining shoes. I made a shoe shine box and filled it with polish and a brush. I also found two good old rags for shining and started my business. I walked the streets to catch the servicemen and talk them into a shine. I charged ten cents but most of the men gave me a quarter.

After a couple of months another a boy by the name of Vic started shining shoes too. This didn't upset me or hurt my business because there was plenty of servicemen. Even though I didn't need to do this I enjoyed the excitement of making my own spending money.

In May 1944, the folks closed the store, shut up the house and moved in with Uncle Jeff, my father's big brother who owned a dairy farm east of Tampa. Jeff's wife had left him so mom took over running the house and we helped Uncle Jeff through this trying period. Living on a dairy farm was a new experience for me.

He had a full time supervisor and six workers. Each family had their own house rent free plus they could have a garden and get free milk. He paid his supervisor $70.00 per month and the workers received $50.00 per month. Most of the help had limited education but they enjoyed working with milk cows. They would milk the cows at 2 A.M. and again at 2 P.M., seven days a week. He milked 250 cows and all their feed came in cotton print sacks which many women would use to sew shirts and dresses for their families.

While we lived there my Uncle Jeff offered to give me each new calf born from his herd, the feed and a pen if I would care for them. But I was too much of a city kid to realize what his offer meant. Of course I didn't accept because of the commitment, it was a lot of work and I knew we'd be moving back home at the end of the summer. I really didn't want to be there anyway because all of my friends were back in Zephyrhills. I couldn't wait until the folks were ready to move back home.

Finally the summer was over and we packed up and went back to our home so I could go back to school. Dad opened the store again and everything was back to normal.

One day my dad said, "James, we need to paint this old truck with a brush so do you feel the job would be too big for you?"

"No dad, I can do it. I think you are right, it has gotten old looking. It may take me several days but I will give it a try." Dad took me to Mr. Curtis' Hardware store and helped select black paint and a brush. He paid Mr. Curtis and we headed home. I did a small portion of the truck at a time which allowed it to dry so we still had use of it. It took me five days before I finally completed the job and it shone like a new truck! Dad was real proud that I could do an important job like this.

Around September, 1944, a new family moved into town by the name of Williams and purchased one of the drug stores. He had two daughters, Bonnie was my age and Gracie was a couple years older. They moved to a house just across the street from the city park. I learned from Bonnie at school that they loved to dance. I wanted to learn modern dancing so the girls said they would teach me.

I showed up at their house at a prearranged time and the girls taught me how to dance the two step. We usually danced to records but sometimes Gracie would play the piano and Bonnie and I would dance. I sure enjoyed the time we spent together and a couple of times I took Bonnie to the movies. In our class I was the only boy who could dance! I never understood why the other guys didn't learn. That made me in high demand at dances and I had a great time. I loved to dance.

There was also a girl in my class whose father and brothers made moonshine. They had a still in the woods which was destroyed when they got arrested and put in jail. But when they got out they would set up another still in a different location and do it all over again.

Mother at back door of house

Powell Ryals standing on the front of a
Deep Sea Fishing boat in Tarpon Springs Florida

Powell and Maude Ryals with son James
in front of business Zephyrhills

Mother holding James age 3 months

James age 5 at swimming pool Zephyrhills

James age 7 at swimming pool Zephyrhills

James holding his dog age 10 in
back yard of his home in Zephyrhills

TEEN YEARS

In the summer of my 13th year I was hired to work at the converted skating rink in town to wash hot peppers to be pickled. They had closed this rink and we had to go to Crystal Springs to skate. I only lasted a month because the peppers were so hot they burned my fingers through my gloves.

Mother was elected President of the Zephyrhills High School PTA the year I entered the 8th grade. She took the job seriously and kept aware of everything going on in the school. It seems like I remember her mentioning the principal received $2500.00 a year salary plus a rent free house. The teachers received $1200.00 to $1500.00 depending on their experience. Sure was different than today.

There was a rumor about a young, single, female teacher who recently was hired to teach in our school. Someone claimed they saw her having a beer in another town at the bar. Zephyrhills did not allow any alcoholic beverages to be sold within the city limits and did not approve of a teacher drinking alcoholic beverages. The community couldn't have their teachers, especially a single female, drinking. That conduct, if it was true, could get her fired! I never heard any more about the situation so it must have been just a rumor.

I really messed up in homeroom one day and my 8th grade teacher, Mr. Thatcher, told me to go out in the hall and to be prepared for a spanking. I told him my mother did not approve of spanking in school and he would be in deep trouble if he put a hand on me. I think I was a bit cocky because mom was President of the PTA.

For some reason he did not spank me. I told my mother what had happened and she went to see Mr. Thatcher. She informed him spanking in this school would not be tolerated. There wasn't any more talk about the incident and all spanking in school ceased. Before this the principle used a paddle when he spanked errant children.

Not long after the Sheriff of Pasco County, who lived in Dade City, came into town on a Saturday afternoon and was asking where Mr. Thatcher lived. I overheard and told him I would show him. I got to ride in the sheriff's car over to Mr. Thatchers. He left me in the car while a couple of people that were there took him out back to the shed. They had found Mr. Thatcher dead of self inflicted cyanide poisoning. I never found out why he killed himself.

One of the most exciting things about being in the 8th grade was now I was able to play varsity sports. Due to the small enrollment in our school 8th thru 12th grades played varsity sports. I wasn't a large kid, in fact, I was 5 ft 6 inches and weighed about 110 lbs. Since our school was small you could play varsity ball and earn a school letter. Each year those who had the required number of playing points received a big letter "Z". I received a total of three playing football and basketball for three years.

Our football practice field in Zephyrhills was just a vacant lot with uneven ground. We never played any games there. At New Port Richie they played their games in a pasture with a few cow pies here and there. You can imagine getting tackled and landing on one of them! Some of the other towns had lights so those games could be played at night otherwise they were played in the late afternoon. In all the years I played football we won only one game. After I moved to Tampa they started winning most of the games. It made me wonder if I had been the problem.

I obtained a drivers learner permit at age 14 and my father and mother took turns teaching me how to drive. The only time I could drive was if another person with an operators license was in the vehicle with me. I started helping the folks deliver furniture on Saturday with dad and old Jack. Jack was still paid 75 cents per delivery!

Around this time a group of us basketball players were upset with the school board who planned to change the surface of our outside basketball court and never mentioned it to us. Like we had any say in it! There was this young man who had been in the military and now returned to school who was hanging out with us. He told us he could get some rotten eggs from his brother's farm to egg the president of the school board's house. We agreed that was a good idea so after he got the eggs he drove us to the president's house where we proceeded to throw the eggs at his house. It was foolish of us to be influenced by this older boy who didn't even play basketball. Of course in a small town we were identified and the policeman arrested us. We had to go to court where the judge sentenced us to wash the egg off the president's house and we were banned from playing basketball for the rest of the season. This not only hurt the team but prevented me from earning more points to obtain another 'letter' in sports. My parents were upset with me but told me I had to be responsible for my actions. Afterwards I realized it was a stupid reason to be mad at the school board. Later, the school board decided not to resurface the basketball court after all.

During this period mom decided we needed to raise chickens and buy a cow. So dad had someone build a chicken yard with a good fence around it and a wooden hut for the hens to lay their eggs and roost in for the night. This same person also made our garage into a cow barn. After it was ready mom went out and bought an old Jersey milk cow who happened to be blind.

Mom knew I didn't know how to milk cows but she asked me to take care of the cow anyway. It took me about a week but I became fair at handling the milking chore. I had to milk old Daisy (I named her) each morning then lead her about five blocks west to a good grazing area. Every evening she was waiting for me at the gate of this pasture and I would lead her to the barn to feed and milk her again. My mother learned how to milk also so when I had a ball game or any other activity in the evening she took care of the cow. Along with milking I had to keep the barn clean which was a dirty job but someone had to do it!

Mom was in charge of the chickens. She bought fifty baby chicks which she kept in the house until they were ready for the yard. These little chickens were to be raised for fryers only. Once the chickens reached about 3 ½ lbs she would hang about ten of them at a time by their feet on the clothes line and then went down the line and cut off their heads. After the blood all ran out she would dip them into a big old iron pot full of boiling water placed in the middle of our yard. The hot water made it easier to pull the feathers off.

The next job was to hold the plucked chicken over another fire she had in the yard to singe off the pin feathers that remained. This was a bit smelly. It was a big job but my mother was skilled at cleaning chickens. After cleaning out the insides she placed them in a tub of ice to chill. Then she wrapped the chickens in butcher paper and would take them to the cold storage locker in the ice house downtown. We always had plenty of fried chicken. In fact, one time mom fried a whole chicken just for me and I made a pig out of myself!

I don't remember all the facts but for some reason we sold the blind cow and bought another cow. Mom made our butter and I was always impressed with how she made it. She would put the cream in a quart jar, put a thick pad on her thigh, started banging the jar on the pad while she turned it. After a while butter was formed! It was lots of hard work but we ate good.

At the beginning of the summer when I was 14 years old I placed an ad in the Zephyrhills News: "Looking for part-time work. Will do anything!" The only response I got from the ad was from a Mrs. Warren who needed her septic tank cleaned. I mentioned the job to my mom and she said, "James if it is honest work it is worth doing."

I contacted Mrs. Warren and said, "Mrs. Warren I will clean your septic tank for $15.00".

She said, "Okay! When can you do the job?"

I answered, "Tomorrow. I'll be there at 9 A.M." I did the job but it sure was dirty and smelly! I had to take a couple baths to get the smell off of me.

Mr. Pete Williams purchased a piece of land about two miles out of town where he planned to build a house. I knew him so when I saw him in town one day purchasing some items from the hardware store I was curious. "Hi, Mr. Williams! What are you going to do?"

He replied, "I'm going to drill for water on my new property. Do you want to help me this afternoon?"

"Yes sir, I would enjoy doing something different."

I went with him to his property and helped him unload the truck. He had an old tractor set up at the drilling site to hook up to a pulley that turned the drill. He had a 25 foot pipe that needed to be carried to the site so he said, "James, grab the other end of this pipe and we will carry it to the drill hole so we can hook it up." I grabbed the other end of the pipe and we started for the hole. On the way the pipe started swaying and I lost control of it. My end of the pipe fell to the ground, bounced up and hit one of my front teeth breaking it. A concerned Mr. Williams came running over to me and took a look in my mouth. He said, "James the tooth broke in half and the nerve is showing. Get in the truck and I will take you to the dentist."

There was only one dentist in our town and luckily he was in the office. He put me into the chair and numbed my mouth. Then he proceeded to remove the nerve and put a temporary crown on the tooth. When he had finished Mr. Williams took me home and explained what had happened to my mother.

I don't remember if Mr. Williams paid the dentist or if my mom had to. I told Mr. Williams it probably would be better if I didn't help with his drilling. He understood and said, "James I am sorry things didn't work out." A month later the dentist put a permanent crown on the tooth and everything was back to normal.

I belonged to the local 4 H Club and one summer we visited the University of Florida at Gainsville for three days. We slept in tents and attended few classes plus they had a swimming contest. I entered four different contests and won first place in three of them. What a fun three days!

Around 1947 mother purchased a small 2 bedroom house from the school board and had it moved to the lot next to our house. She hired a carpenter to make repairs and bring it up to date for a rental property. I was given the task of building the front steps and a 40 foot sidewalk. I hauled sand from the woods to mix with the cement, which saved money. I did the whole job by myself and it turned out rather nice.

When I turned sixteen the first thing I did was to take the test to obtain my drivers license. I was issued the license on Friday and on Sunday the folks told me I could drive downtown and get some ice cream. I was so excited that I could now drive the car anywhere without another licensed driver with me. I diagonal parked in front of the drug store between two cars and got the ice cream. As I was backing out I saw two girls watching me so I tried to show off in front of them. Can you believe it? Well I backed into Mr. Jenkins car but fortunately the damage was minor and there was no damage to our car. You can imagine my embarrassment when I saw the two girls were still watching. Especially since I knew them! I told him to have it fixed and I would pay for it. I went home and told my stepsister, Vivian Logan who was visiting from Tampa, about the accident. She said, "James, I will loan you the money for the repairs and we won't say anything to the folks." What a great sister! My folks never mentioned it to me but I'm sure they knew because there were no secrets in our town.

Dad's health was getting worse so we sold the store in the early part of May 1948, and traded our truck in for a Hudson coupe. Now we only had our savings to live on so I decided to get a job to bring in some regular money. School was out for the summer and I heard Mr. Walker was hiring at the new theater that was being built. They had the walls up so now they had to be finished with plaster. Mr. Barry Walker was in charge of finishing up the project. I went by to ask if there was a job I could do through the summer and part-time starting in September.

"Hi! Mr. Walker, I am James Ryals and I'm looking for work full-time during the summer and then in September I could work afternoons. I will be attending school in the mornings."

He asked me, "James, do you know how to mix mud for plaster?"

"No, but I am a fast learner and would like the chance to learn."

"This job pays 75 cents an hour and during the summer we start at 7 A.M. until 5 P.M., Monday through Friday with an hour for lunch. If you work out, then when school starts you will be working from 1 P.M. to 5 P.M. Monday through Friday and maybe sometimes on Saturday. I will need you to start on Monday. Can you be here?"

"Yes sir, with bells on my shoes," then I gave a big laugh.

He said, "See you on Monday."

"Thanks a million, Mr. Walker!" I replied.

I took off running for home to inform my folks about the job and mentioned I would be able to contribute in a small way to our household. Mom said, "James, we are proud of you but I hope you are not obligating yourself too much. You know you have your schoolwork to keep up and you don't have to help with the finances but it will be deeply appreciated." Mom continued, "James, your dad and I have been wanting to discuss an idea with you. It is something we feel will help solve our income situation in the future and give you a better chance in life."

At this point my dad is 49 years old and being handicapped he needs assistance daily in all his activities while mom at 65 is still full of drive and energy. She wasn't very tall but sturdy built. She was an accomplished pianist and played for the local yearly concerts. She belonged to the local drama club and performed in a couple of stage plays. She also was the only state delegate to the National Women's Club convention in Chicago. She has been the backbone of the family since dad hasn't been able to work.

Mom and dad sat me down at the kitchen table and explained their plans. They had received $3500.00 from a large furniture dealer for our business and now they have someone else who will buy both our houses for $6500.00, which will give us total of $10,000.00. In 1948 that amount of money sounded good but there wasn't any projected income.

Mother talked about the three of us moving to Tampa. She said, "There is a possibility we could buy an apartment house near the University of Tampa and rent sleeping rooms only with no cooking allowed. It must have adequate living quarters on the first floor for the three of us and be in a nice neighborhood. You can attend a large school and improve your chances for a better life. We would like to move during the school's Christmas break and then you could start school in Tampa in January to finish out your school year." Of course like all children moving away from my childhood friends was going to be difficult but I understood why it was necessary and would give it my best effort.

I started working as a plaster helper and learned to mix mud plus other duties. Mr.Walker was a nice guy to work for and sometimes I got some extra hours. The summer seemed to fly by and he arranged for the builder to give me a job in the afternoons after school started. I worked for him up until two weeks before we moved to Tampa. I hated giving up the job but there was nothing I could do.

Mom went to Tampa in November to visit a local real estate office and was able to find the type of property she wanted. It was a large rooming house located within six blocks of the University of Tampa with four furnished rooms upstairs, each having their own bathroom (cooking was not allowed) and our living quarters was downstairs. This was an ideal location to rent to students. My stepsister, Vivian, who was working in Tampa could rent one of the rooms. Mother could purchase this property with a small down payment and low monthly payments.

We contacted the buyer in Zephyrhills and he purchased our two houses for the price that had been agreed upon earlier. Everything was in place for our move to Tampa.

In late December we moved to our new house in Tampa with Vivian joining us as our first renter. My mother's first husband had been an attorney in Chicago and they had had three children, all of them old enough to be my parents. The two boys still live in Chicago but her daughter, Vivian, now lives with us.

I immediately enrolled in Plant High School, the school in my area. I looked around for a part-time job but couldn't find one. So I visited the local barber shop about a block from our house and talked to the owner. I saw he had a big shoe shine stand but no one to work it. I also noticed he had a large machine for pressing clothes.

We talked a while and I convinced him to let me try shining shoes and pressing clothes. We agreed on my share of the revenue and that I would work Saturdays or anytime school was closed.

I worked there during the last part of my 11th grade and during that time mom decided she was not cut out to manage the problems that occurred with the boarders. She located a three bedroom house on the north side of town for only $9,000. She listed our apartment building and fortunately it sold right away. Lucky for us the house was still available after we sold the apartment building. We moved to 200 E. Fern St. on May 27th and I immediately went to my new school, Hillsborough High School, to register for my senior year. I had to give up my job at the barber shop because it was too far away.

That summer, mother read an ad describing a new scrub mop where you squeeze the water out of the mop by turning the handle. The mop head was a sponge and ideal for cleaning the kitchen floor. Most homes in Tampa had linoleum kitchen floors that needed mopping almost daily. These mops would make the task easier and mom sent me out to demonstrate this new style of mop to all of the housewives around our area. I did not know she had purchased 24 of these mops. Once I got into the potential buyers house and demonstrated the mop, the sale was easy. I would write up the order and promised to deliver in three days with payment due upon delivery.

Well I was fortunate because they sold like hot cakes! It took me eight days to sell all of them but I went to mom and pleaded with her, "Please don't order any more of the mops. It wears me out trying to get in the door. Of course once I get in there isn't any problem. But I just don't take the rejections too well."

So she agreed not to purchase any more mops. My mom explained that she had me sell these mops to teach me how to approach the public and not for the little income. Of course the extra money came in handy!

During the early days of my senior year I enlisted in the Florida Army National Guard and was paid for each day there was duty. The amount wasn't much but it was a little extra to help mom out and it gave me some spending money.

I also traveled most of the time via Tampa's bus system so I rarely had to use our vehicle. This kept my transportation cost at a minimum.

Vivian had moved with us to our house and she still paid mom rent but I knew what little extra money I could bring in from a part-time job would be helpful. I applied for a part-time job as a stock boy at MAAS BROTHERS DEPARTMENT STORE on Saturdays and all holidays and was hired. Besides stocking shelves I even learned how to gift wrap items for customers.

My entertainment during this time was attending a movie once a month. Sometimes I went with my mother and Vivian. On Saturday evenings there was free round dancing at the Tampa Recreational Center. I always tried to attend and would dance all evening. There was always plenty of girls from all over Tampa. The local radio station's disk jockey played the music and gave away six packs or larger of Coca Cola after each dance contest that was held. I had many different partners and at least once during the evening one of them and I would win the contest. The rest of the crowd that didn't enter the contest did the voting.

One night the radio station announced a city wide "Fred Astaire and Ginger Rogers" dance contest to be held a few weeks later at the City Recreation Center. I picked a young lady, Rose Marie Brown, for my partner for the contest and we practiced every chance the recreation center doors were open. The night of the contest my mother and Vivian came to watch. The contest had five judges and we had to dance to four different songs. My partner was super and we came out the big winner. Mom and Vivian were so proud!

A few personalized gifts from Fred and Ginger were mailed to us. Our picture was in the local paper and we also received 25 free dance lessons at ARTHUR MURRAY STUDIO.

Rose Marie and I never dated but just danced together. The local disk jockey contacted us shortly after we won and inquired if we would mind dancing on stage at the largest movie theater in Tampa on Saturday mornings. There was no payment but we got plenty of soft drinks to take home and got to see the movie for free. He had a short program prior to the movie where we would dance one number on the stage. We had lots of fun and we performed about eight different times.

Graduation was just around the corner and I didn't have any plans for the future. However, I always felt God had my future charted and something would present itself to me.

Our neighbors are a nice older couple and their daughter is the Director of Public Recreation for the city of Tampa. She has over 22 playgrounds and recreation buildings under her control.

Each place has one or two instructors on duty at all times. I had talked to her often when she would visit her parents. I decided to call her and see if there is a chance of working at one of the parks. To my surprise she said, "James you can start work the first Monday after graduation. You need to come to my office and complete the employment application."

"Thanks a lot Mrs. Atwater. I really appreciate it."

I started working at the various centers as a fill-in and kept rather busy. I worked for the department the rest of May thru June 30th when I submitted my resignation to enter the military.

I must mention how God blessed me back in 1932, when Powell and Maude Ryals visited the Tampa Orphanage and picked me out to be their son. My folks always stressed the importance of being honest and to treat all people with respect. A child could not have had any more loving and caring parents.

I was aware that the near future would require my entering the military. How would my parents survive without my support? I had just graduated from high school and did not possess any skill for making a good income. The job opportunities for me were limited and it concerned me deeply. I realized the pay scale wasn't much in the military but maybe I could send half of my monthly pay home until something else came along. With lots of prayer and a strong belief that God is in charge, I feel something positive will happen.

The Korean War was going badly according to network radio and there was a cry for more people to enlist. There was a rumor the National Guard would be called to active duty in the near future, and that scared me because I did not want to go with my unit. I decided to check with the Air Force recruiter and find out what he could offer. He talked me into enlisting so I went home and filled out the paper work. When I got to the part requiring me to present my birth certificate, I asked my folks for it and they gave me the only copy they had at home in a file.

I took it to the recruiter where he noticed I was still listed as Joseph Gardner, my name before

I was adopted. Somehow the paperwork to change my name did not get filed and that really upset me. So I went to the court house and got a copy of the adoption record, took it to the Hillsborough Birth Certificate office and they corrected the birth certificate so I could enlist.

James age 14

James and Mother on beach in Biloxi, Mississippi

UNITED STATES AIR FORCE

On July 17, 1950, I was sworn in to the United State Air Force as James Arthur Ryals. A couple of days later my folks and Vivian took me to the Atlantic Coastline train station in Tampa. Two buddies from High School and I boarded the train and after we found our seats we stuck our heads out of the window for one more goodbye to our families. The train left at 8 P.M. for the fourteen hour ride to Chicago. There we disembarked and went to Track 12 for the troop train heading for San Antonio, TX.

The trip was going to take eighteen hours and it would stop at almost every station along the way to pick up more recruits. This was going be a real troop train with six cars carrying recruits from many states. No civilians were aboard our train. We were given food vouchers to purchase food on the train plus at cafes at the various stations.

The train arrived at the San Antonio station at 6 A.M. on July 23rd. Sgt. Rivers met us and loaded us on buses to transport us to Lackland AFB. We were taken to an area covered with a couple hundred eight-man tents. We were told to disembark with our luggage and stand in formation. Soon a young man arrived and said, "I am Corporal Daniels and I will be your squad leader during the next 13 weeks." He told us what to expect the rest of the day, then told us to find a tent, leave our luggage and report back in one hour. We were dismissed and headed for the tents where I finally found a vacant cot and flopped down for a while. There was an overflow of new recruits and the two story barracks were full of current trainees so we had to use the tents. Before I returned to formation at 1200 I made a quick stop at the latrine. We immediately marched to the Mess Hall for our first military meal. We were given metal tray-like plates and as we walked down the line each server would dump a big spoon of food on our plate. No matter if the food was mixed together. This was an experience most people dream of.

Ha! That is a joke! After we ate everyone was back in formation and we marched toward the hospital clinic for shots. Next stop was the barber shop and we all had our heads shaved. Everyone was blessed with a super G.I. haircut!

Once everyone had their haircut and returned to formation, Cpl. Daniels marched everyone to the Mess Hall for the evening meal. We were given 45 minutes to eat and then fall back into formation for the march to the tent area. We were informed reveille would be at 0500 (military time) and everyone must be shaved, showered and dressed for formation at 0630. It seemed everything we did was in formation!

I must mention that the influx of new recruits also caused several major problems for the training staff. First was the quarters: new trainees had to sleep in tents for about ten days until a barracks became available. This was in mid July, one of the hottest periods of the year.

Many troops became overheated during this early part of training.

Second was the uniforms: we had to march and do all our training in our civilian clothes because there was not a sufficient number of uniforms in stock. It took about seven days for us to be issued our military uniforms. Basic training taught everyone how to march, dress, take orders without question and to respect our country and fellowmen. The most important day was "PAYDAY"! I stood in a squadron formation (that formation again) while the commander inspected each trainee and we received an hour lecture on the topic of VD. We received this lecture every payday during training and school. Then we got in line according to our last names, walked up to the payroll table, saluted the officer in charge of paying the troops and shouted our names where I finally received my first paycheck of $50.00.

To add a little extra to my funds I washed, ironed, sewed buttons, etc. for other airmen. Many times other trainees needed cash and if I had the money they could borrow say $5 but had to repay me $10 (two for one) which was due next payday.

By the end of six weeks of training everyone was allowed leave time to visit San Antonio on Sunday. That was the only time trainees were allowed to leave the base. The day I was scheduled to go into town it was raining heavily but that didn't stop me from getting off base. I went to town and met a friend of my mothers' and her daughter for lunch. I walked around in the rain all afternoon and got thoroughly soaked. I returned to my wonderful barracks after dark.

Usually the day a trainee graduates from basic he receives orders for his next assignment. Most of the trainees had orders for a unit in Korea for on-the-job training but a few of us lucked out and were selected to attend a specialty school somewhere in the U.S.A.

I was one of the trainees selected to attend an Air Force school at Keesler AFB, in Biloxi, MS with others from my squadron. We were flown there and when we landed everyone was loaded on a bus that drove us to our individual training squadrons. Upon our arrival we were instructed to pick up our luggage and report to the 1st Sgt. inside the orderly room. Each trainee signed in the log book and was directed to a large room to receive a briefing. The 1st Sgt. greeted us and gave a briefing of the do and do nots while in his squadron. We were sent to the supply office next door to pick up our linens and then was directed toward our assigned barracks. My barracks sergeant was SSGT Henry and he met me at the door where he pointed me to my bunk. There were eight new trainees that joined me in this barracks.

Many of us came from southern communities and even though the military did not allow segregation, the acceptance of sleeping, shaving, showering etc. with a black man was difficult to digest. Not only the color but they were from the north! After a few months of living under these conditions, I found out it didn't mean anything and I was able to accept it. However, in Biloxi segregation still existed.

After we dropped our luggage off at our bunks we returned to the barracks chief's room. He gave a full briefing about the rules while waiting to attend class and then more rules for after you started school. We were required to wear our uniforms while performing military duties and attending school. Otherwise civilian clothes were permitted on or off base.

I had arrived at Keesler on October 7, 1950, and would be kept in transit (waiting to start school) until November 14th when I would start school. During this time the squadron duty sergeant assigned us to performing various details such as cleaning pots and pans at the mess hall.

I contacted the supply NCOIC, SSgt. Jordon, and informed him of my super typing skills. I requested permission to work for him as my detail. He agreed and I became a full time supply clerk. Transit trainees are not allowed to go off base, but Sgt. Jordon wanted me to drive him and his buddies back to the base after they had been drinking in town since I didn't drink. So they would put me in the trunk of the car to go off base. Leaving the base was easy, the guards just waved you through the gate. The hard part was getting back on because the guards looked more closely. On the way back about one block from the gate I climbed in the trunk again and since the sergeants were known to the guards they were waved on through. Lucky for us they didn't look in the trunk.

During this period, gambling was wide open in the area. There were slot machines everywhere even at the bus station. Most of the four major hotels and the bars had black jack tables, crap tables, etc.

During the early 50s all of the Radio Operations, Control Tower and several other career skills were taught in the various hangers. My school was in Hanger #4, adjacent to the flight line. Radio Maintenance had brick buildings for their classes.

We fell into formation (there was that formation again) at 0530 and marched to our school which started at 0600. At 1200 hours we got into formation again and marched back to the barracks. After that we were dismissed for the rest of the day. This was done Monday thru Saturday with Sunday being our only free day.

We could go anywhere after our school hours unless we had special detail. Many of us would go by bus to New Orleans on a Saturday afternoon and return before Monday at 0530. If you had a car you usually would gather up several airmen who would pay you $3 each for the trip and head for New Orleans. We would use the bus station in New Orleans for the drop off and pick up location.

Also there was a twelve mile long beach from Biloxi to Gulfport and several restaurants along the way that sold 'all you can eat' for $1.00. One place sold chicken and another one sold spaghetti, etc. Coca Cola and other sofa drinks at this time were only a nickel for a 10 oz bottle. This was a favorite for the servicemen. There were a couple of high price tourist restaurants that had a varied menu but we didn't go there because of the price.

There was a USO club down on beach row. Top entertainers would stop and give a show on Saturday nights. They served free sofa drinks plus a light food buffet. Many of the local young ladies attended and danced with the

GIs. The rule of the house was none of these young women could make dates with any of the servicemen.

When an important entertainer was scheduled I made it a practice to take the opportunity to be there. If I couldn't get a ride I would get a bus from the base for ten cents and it took me to the city bus terminal. From there I would ride to the end of the line where the USO and community dance hall was located. The bus operated about every 30 minutes with the last bus running at midnight.

I was having difficulty during my first six weeks of school and wrote my mother about my frustration with school and made the comment, "I wish I hadn't joined the Air Force!"

One day a couple weeks later I was called to the orderly room by the 1st Sgt. He said, "James are you having any problems?"

"No sergeant, why?"

"The Judge Adjutant General (JAG) office requests you report to Major Bond at 1400 today. Report back to me after the meeting and tell me what they wanted."

"Ok sergeant!"

I reported to the JAG office and was escorted into Major Bond's office. I saluted him and he said, "Airman Ryals sit down." He explained my mother had written a letter to the base commander. She wrote that I was an only child, that my father has Parkinsons disease and they had no income. I was needed at home to take care of them. The base commander had forwarded the letter to JAG and told them to take care of the situation.

Major Bond said, "Airman, I am speaking for the base commander. You can have a general discharge and go home to support your family. Or we will approve them as your dependents and provide them with an allotment."

I was surprised to have an opportunity to support them by an allotment plus they would have medical benefits. Even though I was having a difficult time with my school, I decided to hang in there and work hard to successfully complete the course.

I thanked Major Bond and said, "I would like to stay in and make my family proud of me."

He took me to his secretary and told her to complete the paperwork for Airman Ryals to apply for a dependent allotment for his father and mother. She completed the forms and I signed them. She said, "I will have Major Bond sign these immediately. They should receive their first check within sixty days."

"Thank you very much!" I replied.

I returned to my 1st Sgt. and explained what had taken place. He was very happy for me.

I wasn't too thrilled about mom writing the base commander but in the long run it got good results. That evening I called mom and gave her the news that within sixty days she and dad would get their first monthly check. They would also receive medical care. I suggested she take dad to MacDill AFB to complete the paper work for their military ID.

They received their first check on January 4, 1951. This amount would be sufficient along with my stepsister's rent check to keep them in food and pay the bills.

I truly believe God had his hand in all that took place. I didn't want to enter the service but it was either being drafted or enter the Air Force. The most difficult situation was my parents didn't have anyone to financially take care of them. My mother was the rock in the family. She took care of dad's every need, got me through high school and always had a smile on her face and a positive comment for me. Now my folks will have financial security including free medical care! This gave me great relief since the pressure was removed from worrying about my parents. Now I could concentrate on being a good student and pass the course. The next several months passed by quickly and I received a promotion to Private First Class which made me happy. This gave me a little more spending money.

I applied for a twenty-day leave to visit my folks in Tampa after graduation. But before I graduated, the NCOIC of Operations at the school had me report to him for some instructions. He said, "You have been selected to be an instructor here in our school. After your twenty-day leave you are scheduled to start a four week instructor course which will start August 10th. You will move into the instructor's barracks the day after graduation from radio school."

On July 6, 1951, I successfully completed the Radio Operations Course and moved into the instructor's barracks before I left on furlough. On July 8th I signed out on my 20-day furlough and went to the Greyhound Bus terminal in Biloxi where I purchased a one-way bus ticket to Tampa, Florida. I planned to purchase a used car while at home. I got on the bus and prepared myself for the long twenty hour trip.

When I arrived at the Tampa bus terminal I called mom and she came and picked me up. Once in the car I said, "Mom, I am going to be home for seventeen days and we are going to have fun." I told her about being selected to be an instructor at the school.

Mom said, "James, your dad and I are proud of you but you know I didn't want my son entering the military. Guess I related to the WW I and old Civil War soldiers who appeared to be nothing but drunks and bums."

"Mom, I know this new opportunity will be a challenge because I only have a high school education. Plus I am only nineteen and over half of the class are older with some of them having a college education."

Mother said, "James, I have faith in you and with hard work you can accomplish anything."

The first couple of days I helped around the house and visited with dad. The following Sunday after church I took mom and Vivian out to dinner. Dad wasn't able to go along but he would be okay unattended for a couple of hours. We reminisced and laughed about my growing up years and talked about what had been happening while I was gone. It made me feel good to be able to make my mother and sister happy during the short time I was home.

On Monday I took mom and dad to Zephyrhills and visited a couple of cemeteries. My dad had taken me around to some of the cemeteries when I was growing up and he especially liked to visit our relative's grave sites. Then we visited a few of my parent's friends before we drove back to Tampa. While driving around town I heard about a dance at the American Legion Hall Saturday night that was open to the public. A small band would provide the music and the cost was $2.50 per person which included the refreshments.

I asked mom, "Mom, if I can get my old dance partner to go with me I would like to go to the dance in Zephyrhills Saturday night. Would you mind?"

"No son, go right ahead. We want you to have a good time."

So when we got back to Tampa I contacted Rose Marie Brown and asked her if she would like to go to the dance in Zephyrhills. She agreed and thought it would be exciting to dance together again.

The rest of the week I shopped around town for a used car. I talked to mom about where I could get the money to purchase a car. She said, "James, I will contact the bank and see what arrangements I can make to get you some money." Later that day she told me, "James the bank will let me have $1200 which they will add to my mortgage. My monthly payment will stay the same. Will that be enough to get you a car?"

"Mom, that will be more than I will need. Thanks."

Saturday evening I drove to Rose Marie's house and picked her up for our night in Zephyrhills. "Hi Rose, you look super and will turn some heads at the dance. You know, I don't think any of the folks in Zephyrhills realize that we won the Fred Astaire/Ginger Rogers dance contest so we can show off our stuff tonight."

Rose replied, "Sounds okay with me. Lets go! By the way James, how is the Air Force treating you? I must say you look sharp dressed in that uniform." So during the drive to the dance I filled her in on what had happened to me during the past year.

The dance didn't start until 8 P.M. so we had plenty of time when we got to Zephyrhills. We stopped at one of the drug stores and got us a sandwich. We saw a few people that I knew and I introduced Rose to them. Everyone assumed we were boyfriend/girlfriend but I didn't say anything to the contrary. Finally we went to the Legion Hall and paid for our tickets. We found an empty table near the dance floor but we were still about 30 minutes early so we watched the band set up. Several of my old friends came over and visited with us.

Once the music started Rose and I hit the floor running and did our old dance routines. After about an hour I asked Rose, "Do you mind if I ask a couple of the local girls to dance?"

"No, go ahead. Maybe some of the guys will ask me." After I started dancing with other girls Rose had several young men ask her to dance.

When it was 10:30 P.M. and we had been dancing all evening I said, "Rose, I think it is time we headed back to Tampa."

"Yes, I think you are right. In fact I may fall asleep on the way home. We sure did dance a lot."

We told everyone goodbye and headed back to Tampa. When I pulled up in front of her house I told her, "Rose, thanks a million for a super evening. I will try and give you a call before I go back to the base."

"Good. I'd like that. See you later."

Mom was still up when I got home. "James did you and Rose have a good time?"

"Yes, it was a wonderful time. We danced all evening and I got to see some of my old friends. Well, good night mom. See you in the morning."

"Good night, son."

One morning at breakfast with mother she said, "James, have I ever talked to you about your dad's and my philosophy of life?"

I said, "No, I don't remember our ever discussing it."

"Would you be willing to listen to me as I ramble on a bit this morning?"

"Sure mom. I enjoy having this private time with you."

"James we believe life is like a ship sailing out in the sea. When the water is calm everyone is safe and there is clear sailing. Then suddenly a storm appears and you quickly close all the port holes and hatches to help keep the ship afloat. The crew works hard and gives you the support necessary to ride the storm. Finally the ship is in calm waters and everything is going good again. Don't forget to thank two sources. First, thank God because He is always with you in the good times and bad. Then thank those people who helped you. This is very important because you can't do it alone. Well, I guess I have bored you enough, son. Anyway this is the way your dad and I try to get through our life."

"Mom, I really appreciate what you have told me. I will try and follow your example. I love you mom!"

The last Saturday of my leave I walked with my mother to her German American pinochle party about eight blocks from our house. She was the secretary of this small club which consisted of about thirty men and women over the age of six-five. They played single deck pinochle and everyone had a ball. Mom enjoyed showing me off to her friends. I was willing to be there and that was important to her. I had the low score that night but I didn't care. My mom was happy.

Monday, I took mom to the various used car lots around town to buy a car. We tried several places but they were too expensive or just not the right car. Finally on Florida Avenue about ten blocks from our house I found what I was looking for. The salesman's name was Frank and he showed me a 1948 Fleet Line Chevy sports car with 39,000 miles. It was listed at $1340. I told him

I was stationed in Mississippi and had limited funds. What was the best price he could sell the car for? He went into the office and talked to his boss. When he came back he said, "You can have this car for $1185 cash."

I pulled mother over to the side and she said, "He has a deal if he will wait three hours while we go to the bank to get the money." I repeated what mom had said and he agreed. We headed to the bank where mom signed the papers and we got $1200 cash. We returned to the dealership and completed the paperwork to get my car. On the way home mother drove her car and I followed her to her insurance agent where I insured the car. When we finally pulled up in the driveway at mom's I was the proud owner of a car.

The moment has arrived for me to head back to the base. It seems like I just got home and now must leave. I had such a wonderful furlough and deeply appreciated mother making arrangements for the money I needed to pay for my car.

It is July 25th and I must leave for the base tomorrow morning. It would take me about sixteen hours to get there so I was anxious to get on the road. I got up at 5 A.M. and mom had fixed me breakfast. I went into the bedroom to give my dad a hug and kiss. While I was saying goodbye to dad, Vivian had come into the dining room to say goodbye. I gave mom and Vivian hugs and kisses and headed northwest toward Mississippi.

I arrived back at the base where I unpacked and settled in. The next day was payday so I had to wear my class A uniform for the Commander's formation and briefing. This was my first payday as a regular GI and not a trainee. During the next few days I registered my car and got a new permanent military ID. I had a few days before my Instructor class started so I spent time getting acquainted with the other guys in the barracks.

Also the tires on my car needed to be replaced so I decided to go over to the Sears store at Gulfport. I told the tire clerk what I needed and asked if I could pay for them on time. I had never had credit before, so I didn't know what to expect. Normally the Sears Store policy is a military person must hold the rank of Corporal or higher in order to get their Sears credit card. I was only a Private First Class but because I was going to be an instructor at Keesler they would make an exception. I got my first credit card when I was nineteen and I was thrilled. It made me feel so grown up.

Now that I have transportation I decided to locate a church to meet the local folks and participate in their senior youth activities. I decided to visit several churches with some of my friends and we finally found a small Baptist Church in rural Gulfport. I started going to Sunday School, church and evening services. I became close friends with Bill and Alice Rodgers. Bill was a deacon and Alice was a Sunday school teacher. One Sunday before church Bill said, "Jim would you like to have dinner with us after church?"

"Bill I would like that very much."

I had become friends with their three children during the youth activities. Lois was 18 and starting college at the Mississippi Women's

College at Hattiesburg. Judy was 16 and their son, Ralph, was 14. They both attended Gulfport high school.

Bill had been a railroad conductor and retired last year. Alice was a homemaker and active in the community. Several times on Saturday night I spent the night on the couch and would hang out with the family all day Sunday. I was like a big brother to the kids!

I reported to Building 2008 at 7 A.M. on August 10, 1951, for my first day of a four-week course at the Instructor's school. We were welcomed by Major Dunn, Officer in Charge of the school. Then he introduced MSGT Harry Robertson as the main instructor who introduced the other instructors and identified the subjects each of them would teach. Of course I was keeping notes of his briefing.

MSGT Robertson clarified that our school hours were from 7 A.M. to noon Monday through Friday. He mentioned both the Dale Carnegie training and Toastmasters International, whose motto is "Where Leaders are Made." He was clear that this course was designed along those lines.

Our class consisted of ten students from all different backgrounds. I was the youngest and the only person who had completed the Radio Operations course. There are two Staff Sergeants who just completed the Control Tower course. Each of these men had a college degree and once held the rank of captain at the end of WW II. Another one was a MSGT who was called back into the service to be an instructor for the Electronic Maintenance course. He sold his TV repair business when he was recalled. The other six men had completed the Radar Maintenance course and would return to that school to be instructors.

We spent many hours on how to prepare for 2, 5 and 15 minute lectures. During the course each student was selected spontaneously to give various timed lectures. We were given many topics to prepare for these lectures. For example: the instructor would say, "Airman Ryals, give a two minute lecture on operating a radio." I would reach in my brief case and select the time and subject cards for that presentation. Each student was graded on each of their lectures.

I spent many hours in the base library to set up the various lectures and planned to always be prepared for the unexpected. I found the course extremely interesting and felt an honor to be part of this group.

One Saturday morning while sitting around the barracks with Jake, a barracks roommate, he and I were talking about our youth and the different things we experienced in our life while growing up.

"I remember while growing up in Zephyrhills, Florida, my family did not have a telephone at home or in dad's furniture store. There may have been ten phones in the whole town and some of them were at city hall, the doctor's office, the post office and the drug store. My first experience with a telephone was when my family moved to Tampa and we had a phone in our home. To make a call you picked up the receiver and a telephone operator answered by asking, 'Switchboard. What number are you calling, please?' You would give the operator a number like Madison 6767 or Pacific 9989 and the telephone operator would contact your party. It took me a while to get used to it but I finally did. It certainly was convenient. Now I can call mom if I want to."

Jake said, "We still don't have a phone in our home in Maryland. It sure would be nice to be able to call home."

It was getting around lunch time when I said, "Jake, I have to go over to Gulfport to the Sears store. Do you want to come along and we could grab a hamburger on the way?"

"Sure, it's better than hanging around the barracks all day." So Jake and I headed to Gulfport and stopped at a hamburger joint along the beach.

Once we got to Gulfport I drove over to the Sears store and made my purchase. Afterwards we just walked around town and looked in the store windows.

One of the larger stores had an ad displayed about the new TVs. "Look Jake, a TV set! I haven't ever seen a TV before. Wow! The ad says they want $1599.00 for it. Can you believe that? I don't even know anyone that has one, do you?"

"No, I don't think we have any in my rural county. I live in a small town in Maryland. Who could afford to buy one anyway?"

The store had the speakers hooked up outside so those looking through the window could hear the program that was being broadcast on the TV. I said, "It's like watching a movie screen except smaller. Well, since you aren't going to buy the TV for me I guess I will still take you back to the barracks. Hahaha!" Finally we had to return to the base for evening chow. It turned out to be a fun afternoon.

What a surprise when six months later each squadron got a TV for their day room!

After many hours of studying and attending school I finally reached graduation day. On that day Major Dunn gave his final speech. After we all received our certificates the Major called me up to the front and presented me with the Honor Student award. That was a shock and I smiled from ear to ear with pride.

Immediately following graduation I called my folks with the good news about graduating and receiving an award for being an Honor Student. Mom said, "James we are so proud of you and we love you very much. We knew you could do it."

"Me too mom, and tell dad I love him and I love you too. You are both in my prayers every day."

Now I am ready for the challenges of my new career.

How blessed I am that Powell and Maude Ryals had decided to make me a part of their family. And now you know what has happened to orphan Joseph Gardner!

By James A. Ryals and Carol S. (Ochsner) Ryals